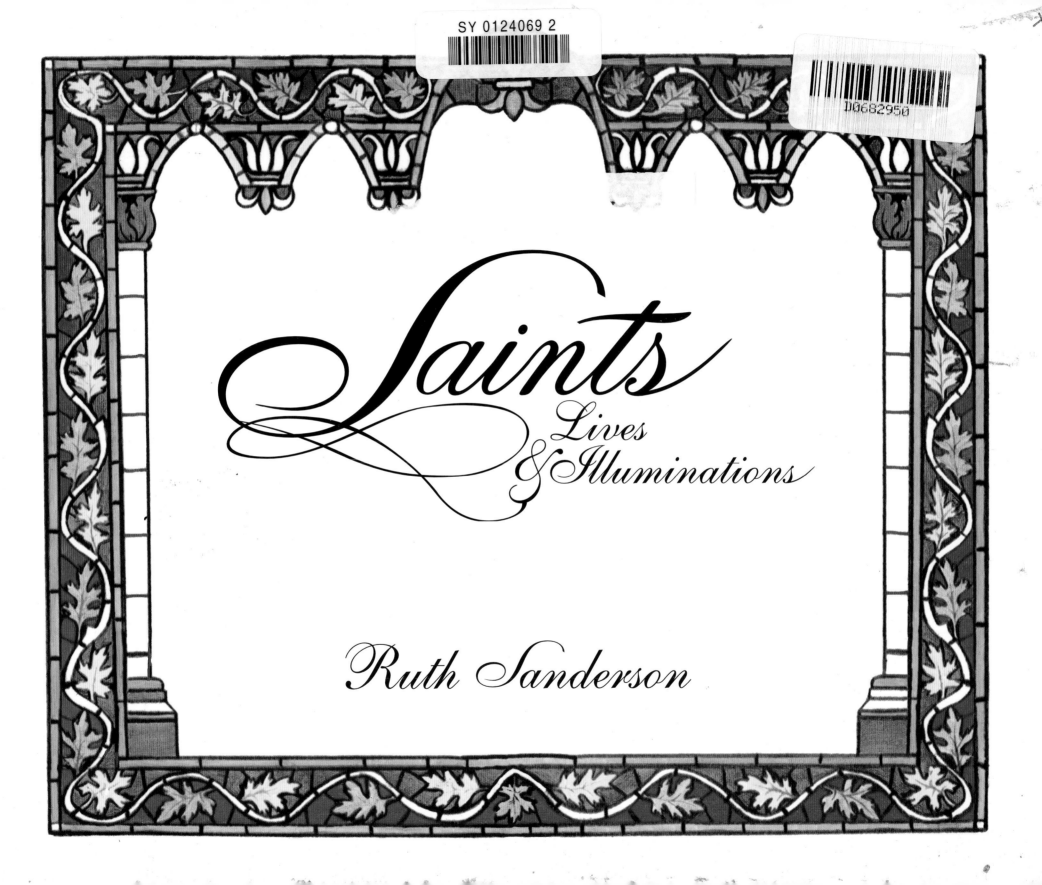

Saints
Lives
& Illuminations

Ruth Sanderson

Published 2003 by Eerdmans Books for Young Readers
An imprint of Wm. B. Eerdmans Publishing Company
2140 Oak Industrial Dr. NE, Grand Rapids, MI 49505
P.O. Box 163, Cambridge CB3 9PU U.K.

07 08 09 10 11 12   7 6 5 4 3 2

Library of Congress-in-Publication Data
Sanderson, Ruth.
Saints : lives and illuminations, the first millennium / Ruth Sanderson.
p. cm.
Summary: Privides brief stories from the lives of forty Christian
saints of the first millennium.
978-0-8028-5220-5 (hardcover : alk. paper)
978-0-8028-5332-5 (paper: alk. paper)
1. Christian saints—Biography—Juvenile literature. [1.Saints.]
I. Title.
BR1711.S26 2003
270'.092'2—dc21
[B]
2002009083

The illustrations were rendered in pencils and oils on paper.
The display type was set in modified Vivace.
The text type was set in Venetian.
Book designed by Matthew Van Zomeren.

For Father John Daly

Saint Stephen

First Century

Stephen was one of the seven deacons appointed by the apostles to aid the poor and to help govern the first Christian community. He spoke with such wisdom that the ranks of disciples in Jerusalem grew and grew. The elders of a certain synagogue plotted against Stephen. They falsely charged him with blasphemy against Moses and God.

Stephen was brought before the Sanhedrin, and he gave a long defense of Christ's teachings. They did not pay attention to his words. Stephen knew he was going to be killed.

Filled with the Holy Spirit, the brave young man looked up and saw a beautiful vision of Christ sitting at the right hand of the Father in the heavens. He was then sentenced to be stoned to death.

Before he died, Stephen prayed aloud that the sins of his murderers not be held against them. Wild beasts kept watch over his body until his friends came and took it to be buried in an unmarked grave. Centuries later a priest was told by an angel that he would be able to find the grave of Saint Stephen by the beautiful red roses that bloomed next to it, and so it happened.

Stephen was the first Christian martyr. He is the patron saint of Hungary, Poland, bricklayers, and stonemasons.

Saint Christopher

FIRST CENTURY

Christopher was a giant of a man, massive and powerful. He wanted to find the greatest king on earth so that he might serve him. Deciding at first that the devil was the most powerful and greatest king, he went out to serve him. Then he realized that the devil fled from any sign of Christ, and Christopher became determined to seek Christ instead.

Christopher met a hermit who taught him the Christian faith. Then he told Christopher to go to a certain river and to help people with the dangerous crossing. So Christopher built a hut by the river and made a great staff to help him keep his balance in the water. One stormy night he heard a child's voice calling him.

Christopher took the child up onto his shoulders and entered the river. The weight of the child grew and grew, and Christopher struggled mightily to reach the opposite bank. Then he said to the child that he felt as if the weight of the whole world were on his shoulders.

The child replied that Christopher had borne the weight of the One who had created the world, for he was none other than Christ, the King whom Christopher served. The child told Christopher to plant his staff next to his hut, and the next morning the staff had turned into a tree bearing fruits and flowers.

Christopher traveled to Lycia and was soon imprisoned for his beliefs, for many Christians were being martyred in that city. He refused to renounce his faith and make sacrifices to the pagan gods. Many people were converted to faith in Christ before Christopher was beheaded.

Christopher is the patron saint of travelers of all kinds.

Saint Lawrence

THIRD CENTURY

About two hundred years after Stephen was martyred, Lawrence was serving as a deacon. This was a dangerous position, for, depending on who was in power, Christians were often persecuted. When Valerian became emperor, he ordered the Pope, Sixtus II, put to death. Then he made plans to have all bishops, priests and deacons killed as well. Valerian hoped that if the flock of Christians had no shepherds, they would hopefully scatter.

Before his death, the Pope had told Lawrence to sell all the Church's treasures and give the money to the poor. While Lawrence was carrying out his order, the prefect got word about the Church's wealth. He sent for Lawrence and demanded that he turn over all the Church's property.

Lawrence asked for three days to gather everything together, saying that he would show the prefect riches exceeding all the wealth in the royal treasury. After the prefect left, Lawrence continued to distribute the wealth of the Church to the needy.

Three days later, Lawrence called together the poor, the sick, and all those who lived through the charity of the Church. He presented these people to the authorities and said, "Here are the treasures of the Church." The emperor was outraged when the prefect told him what had happened, and he ordered Lawrence to be tortured and killed.

Lawrence endured his torture with good humor and even made jokes before his death. He is the patron saint of the poor.

Saint Catherine

THIRD CENTURY

Catherine of Alexandria was a noblewoman well known for her beauty and intelligence. She studied the great works of Plato, Homer, and Aristotle. Though many men desired to marry her, none met her ideal. When she learned from a hermit that only Christ possessed the qualities she was searching for—compassion, wisdom, wealth and beauty—Catherine was baptized a Christian and dedicated her life to Christ.

Catherine spoke out eloquently in public in defense of the Christian faith. She also condemned the pointless slaughter of animals in sacrifice to pagan gods. Many people were converted to Christianity after hearing her speak.

Even Emperor Maxentius was captivated by Catherine's majestic stature and self-assurance. He ordered the most learned of Greek scholars to come and debate with Catherine and show her the "error" of her thinking. But Catherine would not be defeated. When she refused to renounce her beliefs, the emperor became enraged. He had Catherine thrown into prison.

Before Catherine was put to death, the Emperor's own wife was converted, and she too was later executed for her belief. Catherine was tied between great spiked wheels, but it is said that lightning struck the wheel and saved her from this torture. Catherine was then beheaded, and milk, not blood, flowed from her body.

Catherine is one of the Fourteen Holy Helpers, a group of saints who have proven particularly helpful when invoked in times of great difficulty.

Saint Cecilia

Cecilia was born into a wealthy Roman family. When she became a teenager, her family arranged her marriage to a nobleman named Valerian, a pagan who worshiped idols. Cecilia was not happy, for she wished to be only the bride of Christ.

When Cecilia poured out her heart in prayer to God, an angel appeared to her and said, "Do not be afraid to marry. Tell your husband what you desire, and I will be there to protect you."

On their wedding night, Cecilia confessed to Valerian that she wished to remain a maiden and that her guardian angel was there to protect her. "Can I see this angel?" he asked. She told him to go to Bishop Urban, who would teach him how he could have an angel, too.

God touched Valerian's heart. He understood that the pagan idols he had worshiped were just pieces of stone. Bishop Urban baptized Valerian, and he was blessed with the vision of his own guardian angel standing next to him. He rushed back to Cecilia.

When Valerian entered the room, he heard music so divine that his heart filled with joy. An angel stood next to Cecilia and put a crown of flowers on her head.

Valerian and his brother, Tiburtius, became very active doing good works, and burying Christian martyrs. Then, they were arrested and put to death.

Cecilia taught many people in her home about the faith. Bishop Urban baptized hundreds of people there. Eventually, when word reached the governor, she was arrested, tortured, and beheaded.

Cecilia is the patron saint of musicians and singers.

Saint Barbara

Barbara's father, Dioskoros, hated Christians. In order to keep his daughter from learning about Christianity, he built a beautifully furnished tower for her to live in. There Barbara had plenty of servants, as well as tutors in many subjects, but she was only allowed in the small enclosed yard next to the tower and could go no further. Yet her father's plan failed, for one of Barbara's tutors was secretly a Christian, and soon she believed as well.

It happened that Dioskoros hired workers to build a bathhouse with two windows next to Barbara's tower. Then he departed on business. While he was gone, Barbara told the workers to add a third window. When her father returned, he was surprised to see three windows instead of two.

When Dioskoros questioned her, Barbara admitted that she had changed his order, saying she thought the bathhouse would look better with three windows. He asked her why.

"Three windows illuminate everyone who comes into the world," she said. Then she made the sign of the cross and added, "For the Father, the Son, and the Holy Spirit light up the whole universe."

Though Dioskoros had loved his daughter, he hated her now that she was a Christian. He drew his sword to kill her, but Barbara ran and escaped into the mountains. When a shepherd betrayed her to her father, she was arrested, tortured, and sentenced to death. Her father struck her down with his own sword. A moment later, he himself was struck down by a bolt of lightning.

Barbara is the patron saint of builders and architects.

Saint Ephraim

FOURTH CENTURY

Although Ephraim's father was a pagan priest in Syria, he was raised as a Christian by his devout mother. He studied all aspects of the Christian faith, as well as philosophy, but his talent in writing and music soon became apparent.

Ephraim's teacher and friend, Bishop Iakovas, tonsured him a monk and ordained him as a deacon. Ephraim became director of a theological school in Syria, and he earned a world-wide reputation as a teacher, lecturer, writer, and hymnographer.

During the time of the persecution of Christians, Ephraim took refuge in a community in Edessa. He spent most of his time living in a cave, writing praises to God in the form of hymns and prayers. Because of the beautiful quality of his hymns, the people there referred to him as "The Lyre of the Holy Spirit." The lyre is a beautiful musical instrument whose sound resembles the harp—melodious and angelic.

As well as writing sacred music, Ephraim spent time creating an organization to help the victims of famine, a great problem in those times.

Ephraim was one of the most gifted contributors to prayer and hymnography in the history of the Christian Church. Many of his hymns and prayers are still used in Orthodox churches today.

In 1920, Pope Benedict XV decreed that Saint Ephraim the Syrian be listed among the Fathers of the Church for his great accomplishments.

Saint Spyridon

FOURTH CENTURY

A humble shepherd who could not read, Spyridon was brought up by devout Christian parents on the island of Cyprus. Spyridon memorized the church services and most of the holy scriptures. The bishop of the area was so impressed by Spyridon's character that he ordained him a priest as a young man.

As the years passed, Spyridon gained a reputation for helping people in time of need. Through his prayers droughts were ended, the blind could see, and the sick were healed. He became a shepherd of men, guiding his flock in the faith. When he himself became afflicted with blindness, he simply considered it a gift from God.

Once, Spyridon sold some rams to a nearby farmer. Spyridon told the man to put the money in a certain place and to take the rams. Seeing that Spyridon had not counted the money, the farmer decided to take an extra ram. Halfway home the ram turned around and ran back to Spyridon's stable. This happened three times. After the farmer confessed his crime and paid for the extra ram, it followed him home willingly.

In his later years, word spread of Spyridon's charity, humility, and wisdom. Though he was uneducated, he was invited to the great meeting of the Fathers of the Church, the First Ecumenical Council. Again and again his opinion was sought after, for though he was blind, his inner vision was sharp.

Spyridon is a much beloved saint in Greece.

Saint George

FOURTH CENTURY

George was a Christian who became an officer in the Roman army. The most famous story about Saint George is his encounter with a dragon. Some believe this episode was added to his story in later years. Even so, it can be seen as a symbolic tale of his fight against the devil, who is symbolized by a serpent or a dragon.

George discovered that a dragon was terrorizing the countryside near a certain city. The people had placated it by offering a daily sacrifice of sheep. Then they began to offer it human sacrifices. On the day that George arrived, the lot had fallen to the King's daughter. She was tied near the entrance of the dragon's cave to meet her fate. But the dragon was not to have his meal that day.

The brave knight engaged the dragon in battle with sword and lance until it was subdued. Then he put a rope around its neck and led it back to the city. George offered to slay the beast if the people became Christians. The king agreed, and all the people were baptized. George told him to give the reward money to the poor.

George's most courageous act was when he stood up to the Emperor Diocletian. George boldly spoke out in public against the pagan gods. He was arrested and endured terrible tortures before being beheaded and glorified as a martyr of the Christian faith.

During the Crusades of the Middle Ages, the life of Saint George was a model for Christian knights. His story was especially popular in England, and he became known as the Protector of the Kingdom.

Saint Alexandra

The Roman Emperor Diocletian was responsible for the imprisonment and torture of many Christians. His wife, Alexandra, however, was admired for her consideration for others. She was extremely popular with his subjects.

During a tour of inspection for the state, Alexandra became aware of the plight of a former Roman soldier. This was none other than Saint George, who was being tortured for refusing to worship the pagan gods. Something compelled Alexandra to visit this prisoner.

Saint George told the Empress that his wounds were nothing compared with his love of Christ. She was astonished that he could be so calm when he was tortured so brutally. Hearing his assurance that he was well content to suffer for Christ, Alexandra began to wonder about this Messiah, this Christ. It was not long before she too came to believe.

The Empress Alexandra rushed back to her husband, Diocletian, to beg him to have mercy on George. The Emperor thought she had taken leave of her senses. When she kept insisting on a pardon, Diocletian saw that she had been won over by the Christians.

Though it was his own wife he was condemning, the Emperor did not hesitate. He ordered Alexandra to be cast into prison, where he planned to behead her along with Saint George. That night, however, Alexandra died in her sleep. A few days later Saint George was beheaded.

Saint Martin of Tours

FOURTH CENTURY

It was a bitterly cold winter day when Martin, a young soldier in the Roman army, came upon a shivering beggar. He cut his cloak in half with his sword and gave half of it to the man. That night, Martin dreamed of Christ dressed as the beggar in Martin's cloak. Martin took this as a sign.

Shortly after, Martin was baptized, but he still served as a soldier for a few more years. When he was finally released from service, he was eager to serve God instead.

Martin became a priest and a missionary under the direction of Saint Hilary in France. A number of times he was attacked while tearing down pagan temples, but his attackers were always miraculously stopped from making the fatal blow. He built parishes far and wide and started the first monastery in France. The sick came to him, and so many were healed that he became known as a wonder-worker.

Martin was a humble man, and when he was made Bishop of Tours, he continued to dress and live very simply. Once while he was traveling alone on foot, Martin met a long mule-train pulling an official carriage of the Treasury. The mules were startled by Martin's flowing black robe, and it got tangled in their traces. The officials jumped to the ground and angrily began to beat Martin, leaving him lying in a faint.

When they had untangled the mules, no amount of whipping could get them to budge. When the officials discovered that it was the Bishop of Tours they had just beaten, they begged Martin to forgive them. When Martin gave the officials his blessing, the mules went forward willingly.

Martin is the patron saint of France and soldiers.

Saint Dorothy

FOURTH CENTURY

Dorothy of Cappadocia was the daughter of two martyrs. She was well known for her great devotion to Christian teachings. When the Roman governor ordered her to make a sacrifice to the pagan gods, she refused and he had her tortured.

The governor was reluctant to order the death of such a beautiful, young girl. He sent two sisters who had renounced Christianity to try to persuade Dorothy to turn away from Christian ways. Instead, when the two women spoke to Dorothy, her great faith inspired them to become Christians again.

The governor was infuriated when he found out. Now, he showed no mercy. He ordered all three to be thrown into prison and forced Dorothy to witness the execution of the two sisters.

As Dorothy was led through the streets to her own death, she was mocked by a lawyer named Theophilus who was standing in the crowd. He laughed at her and asked her to send him flowers and fruits when she reached heaven. Dorothy said that she would.

While she was being tortured, the governor noticed such a joyful look upon her face that he asked her how she could be so happy. "Because," she said, "soon I shall be rejoicing with the angels in heaven."

After her death, an angel disguised as a young boy delivered a basket to Theophilus, the man who had mocked her. There were three apples and three red roses in it. He was astonished, for it was the middle of winter, when neither flowers nor fruit could possibly be growing. Theophilus was converted and baptized and later became a martyr as well.

Dorothy is the patron saint of florists and gardeners.

Saint Anthony

FOURTH CENTURY

Anthony was raised in a wealthy Christian family. When he was eighteen, Anthony heard a sermon that inspired him to sell all his worldly possessions and go live in the desert. There he found his heart's desire—solitude—and time to meditate and pray with no attachment to earthly things.

Over the years many men heard of his spiritual life and came to him to follow his example. He guided their spiritual paths, and these men soon became the foundation of the first Christian monastery. Saint Anthony is known today as the father of monasticism.

After Anthony cured a soldier's daughter, more and more people flocked to the monastery seeking his aid. Eventually, Anthony grew weary of the constant demand on his time. He found peace once more when he left the monastery and settled alone on a remote mountaintop.

Anthony wove mats from palm leaves. He planted a garden so he would not be dependent on anyone for his survival. When wild animals damaged his crops, Anthony caught one of them and spoke to it. From that time on his crops grew unharmed.

Anthony left his mountaintop to give courage to the Christian prisoners during the time of the persecution. He then organized another monastic community on the Nile before retreating to his mountain. Still, many people made the difficult journey to see Anthony and later reported cures and miracles. Even the Emperor, Constantine the Great, wrote and asked the advice of this wise monk.

Anthony lived to the age of one hundred and five.

Saint Nicholas

FOURTH CENTURY

Nicholas became a priest at a very young age. When he inherited his parent's wealth, he vowed to use it for charity.

A wealthy man in Nicholas's parish had lost all of his money. He had three daughters and no dowry to offer, so he could not find husbands for them. Becoming desperate, the man was ready to sell his own daughters for money. When Saint Nicholas heard of his plight, he went secretly to the man's home at night and threw three bags of gold through the window.

When Nicholas became Bishop of Myra, the Emperor Diocletian came to power and Christianity was forbidden. Soon Bishop Nicholas and his parishioners were thrown into prison, chained, and tortured. After Diocletian died, Constantine came to power, ordered the release of all Christian prisoners, and Nicholas was freed. During the rest of his lifetime Saint Nicholas performed many miracles, healing the sick and helping people in distress.

Once when he was on a ship bound for Jerusalem to visit Christ's tomb, a fierce storm arose. Nicholas prayed to God, and the storm immediately subsided. Saint Nicholas has appeared to many ships' captains over the years and led them to safety.

Nicholas is the patron saint of sailors and children. He is known to many as Father Christmas because of his love for children and his generous spirit. He is also the patron saint of Russia.

Saint Constantine & Saint Helen

FOURTH CENTURY

Before an important battle, the Emperor Constantine saw a cross of light in the sky inscribed with Latin words saying "In this sign you shall conquer." Though Constantine was not yet a Christian, many of his troops were. He was victorious and went on to become ruler of the entire Roman Empire. Under his rule, Christians were no longer persecuted, and Christianity was an officially accepted religion. Constantine was the one who declared Sunday to be a public holiday.

Constantine moved the capital of the Roman Empire from Rome to Byzantium, and eventually the city was renamed Constantinople. Constantine spent large sums of money on churches and on institutions for the poor. His mother, Helen, a British princess and devout Christian, was his closest advisor. Constantine was baptized and became the first Christian Emperor and one of the greatest.

When Helen was eighty years old she made a pilgrimage to Jerusalem. She hoped to discover the actual cross of Christ, for in a dream she had seen the place where it was buried. When she arrived at Golgotha, she searched for a spot covered with the fragrant basil plant. An excavation unearthed three crosses. To discover which one was the Cross of Christ, the three crosses were brought to a hospital. One by one the crosses were held over the sick, and the one which healed was pronounced the true cross.

Helen oversaw the construction of many beautiful churches in Jerusalem at the sites of major events of Christ's life.

Saint Nina

Nina was a Christian girl who lived under the rule of Constantine and Helen. One night Nina had a dream in which Mary, the mother of Jesus, came to her and said, "Go to the lands in the north and preach the gospel." Then Mary picked a branch of a vine and fashioned a cross from it, saying, "By the power of this cross you will be able to overcome foes and preach your message." When Nina awoke, the cross was in her hand.

Nina traveled for many weeks through mountains full of bandits, bears, and wolves, finally arriving in the land of Iberia (now the Republic of Georgia). Some friendly Jewish people took her in, and she learned the Iberian language from them.

Once Nina watched a huge procession of people make their way to a temple on the top of a mountain. There they worshiped in front of a statue of a pagan god clothed in golden armor and encrusted with jewels. Nina prayed for this false god to be thrown down. All at once, black clouds formed overhead. The people ran to escape the thunder, lightning, and huge hailstones that rained down, destroying the temple and pagan idols.

After this, people began to visit Nina. She taught them about Christianity. Through her prayers, many sick people were healed. One day the queen herself came to visit, for she was quite ill. When Nina made the sign of the cross over her with her vine-branch cross, the queen was healed. She and the king were so impressed with Nina's holiness that they asked Emperor Constantine to send priests to baptize the people.

Nina continued traveling and preaching for the rest of her life, and she is still honored today as the "mother of Georgia."

Saint Basil

FOURTH CENTURY

Basil was blessed with a very sharp mind. For years he studied rhetoric, logic, mathematics, astronomy, medicine, and law. After all of this, he began to study the lifestyles of monks in the Holy Lands.

After visiting monks in Egypt, Palestine, Mesopotamia, and Syria, he felt more drawn to the monastic life than to all his worldly studies. When he returned to his home in Cappadocia, he built a hut on the river Iris, became a priest, and, not long after, a bishop.

Even though he had poor health, Basil started a number of monasteries. He drew up rules for the monks living in the desert as well, for some insincere monks were really no better than thieves and preyed on the local people for food and provisions yet did not lead Christian lives.

Basil had a kind and sympathetic soul and was a truly humble leader. When necessary he engaged in battle against the enemies of the Church. Basil wrote many books as well as a divine liturgy which is still celebrated ten times a year.

By his good example Basil taught his people how to be generous. With his own fortune, Basil constructed a village for the poor which had a hospital, homes for poor widows, an orphanage, and free inns for poor travelers. He was the first bishop to send representatives all over the country to collect contributions for the poor, as well as for people suffering from natural disasters such as earthquakes and floods.

Basil was a wonderful preacher, often speaking to crowds "as vast as the sea," and deserved his title "Doctor of the Church."

Saint John Chrysostom

Fourth Century

Many of the saints were gifted speakers, but only one was called "Chrysostom," which means "golden-mouthed."

John studied oratory and law in Antioch. Then he joined a mountain community of monks and studied the scriptures for four years. Returning to Antioch, he became a deacon and then a priest.

John's sermons were so moving that it was said he could make rocks cry. His church was always filled, with non-Christians as well as Christians, and the common people especially loved him. Then John was elected Patriarch of Constantinople.

John often spoke against the rich classes that flaunted their wealth and ignored the many poor widows and orphans living in the streets. He criticized Empress Eudoxia for her extravagant lifestyle. She and the wealthy courtiers hated him. They secretly plotted and brought false charges against him. The emperor removed him from office and banished him from the city.

On the night John was exiled, when he had gone just a few miles, an earthquake shook the city. People began to riot, clamoring for his return. The empress grew frightened, and John was recalled. He was met by joyful crowds of his loyal supporters.

Empress Eudoxia was still determined to be rid of John. She had a huge statue of herself built outside his church, and when he spoke against it, she succeeded in banishing John permanently from Constantinople. The power of his words, however, could not be banished, even though he died in exile.

Many of John's writings have survived to this day and continue to be greatly treasured. Every Easter in Orthodox churches a sermon of his is read as it was written fifteen hundred years ago.

Saint Paula & Saint Jerome

FOURTH CENTURY

Jerome studied Latin and Greek in Rome and later learned Hebrew after becoming a monk. Jerome was at his best when he was writing and translating, for he loved to argue and made many enemies due to his quick tongue and sarcastic wit. He spent five years alone in the desert to combat his passionate nature.

Jerome became secretary to Pope Damasus and began the task of creating a standard Latin version of the Bible. During his three-year stay in Rome he became the spiritual director of a group of pious Roman ladies, mostly widows. Paula was one of them.

Paula was very rich but gave much of her wealth to help the poor. She and the other widows wanted to enter into monastic life, so they followed Jerome to Bethlehem. There he built both a monastery for men and a convent for women. Paula used the last of her wealth to build a hospital for traveling pilgrims. Paula helped Jerome with his studies, for she was well educated. Jerome helped her as well by teaching Paula's granddaughter.

Once Jerome heard a lion roaring in pain outside the monastery. He discovered that thorns were embedded in the great beast's paw. When he removed them, the lion became as tame as a dog and lived near the monk for some time.

Saint Moses

FOURTH CENTURY

Moses was an Ethiopian slave whose early life was full of hatred and violence. He was a giant of a man and loved to show off his strength by picking fights. Moses was a thief as well, and when his master could not break his unruly spirit, he released Moses from bondage.

Freedom did not bring happiness to Moses. He formed a band of robbers and lived by preying on the weak. His great strength and daring were made legendary in songs about his deeds, and travelers soon were afraid to pass through his territory.

One day when his provisions were low, he decided to raid a nearby monastery. When he entered, Moses met the calm gaze of the abbot. Something in that holy man's manner made Moses pause. He looked into the old man's eyes and knew that the old man could see all the wickedness in Moses's heart. And yet the abbot looked upon the former slave with love, not fear or hatred. Moses felt his hard heart start to melt, and he began to regret the evil deeds he had done.

Moses stayed in the monastery and gave up his life of violence. He prayed for forgiveness. He decided to make up for his past crimes by becoming a monk and bringing the word of Christ to others. He converted his own gang of thieves.

These former criminals became an army of Christian monks, spreading the word of Christ to thousands. Saint Moses founded one of the greatest monasteries of the fourth century. At the age of eighty-five, Moses suffered a martyr's death when his monastery was attacked by barbarians.

Saint Monica & Saint Augustine

FIFTH CENTURY

Augustine was raised in North Africa by his devout Christian mother, Monica, but he did not accept Christianity as a youth. Vain and ambitious, he became a great scholar and philosopher and founded schools for grammar and rhetoric.

During this time Monica constantly prayed for his conversion. Augustine applied for a teaching post in Milan where he met a bishop, the wise Saint Ambrose. Augustine attended his sermons and slowly became convinced of the truth of Christianity.

Augustine was thirty-three years old when Ambrose baptized him on Easter. When Augustine returned to Africa to visit his mother, the blessed Saint Monica told him that all her hopes in the world had been fulfilled. She had never given up on her son. She died shortly thereafter.

Augustine went on to serve as Bishop of Hippo for thirty-five years. The money collected in his church was used to help the poor and to buy the freedom of slaves. Augustine was known to be friendly and affectionate, and often he would invite non-Christians to dinner.

Augustine wrote many books and essays and was a great philosopher. Once, while he was walking by the ocean pondering the meaning of the Trinity, he saw a boy who was trying to scoop the ocean into a hole in the sand with a ladle. It would be easier to do that, he thought, than to truly grasp the nature of God.

Augustine is a Doctor of the Church and is the patron saint of theologians.

Saint Patrick

Patrick was born in a small town in Scotland. When he was a boy, he was kidnapped by barbarians and dragged off to Ireland.

Young Patrick was sold as a slave. For many years he herded sheep, going hungry and enduring cold in the rain and snow. But Patrick felt the presence of God with him, and he felt comforted and full of hope. He learned the language of the Irish people and grew to love them.

One night Patrick heard a voice in a dream saying, "Your ship is ready to take you home." Patrick found the ship and the reluctant captain agreed to take him to Scotland. After they landed, Patrick traveled for weeks and ran out of food. He prayed, and suddenly from over a hill a herd of swine came running to him.

When at last he reached a monastery, Patrick stayed there for two years, working and praying. When he finally went home to his parents, he was a grown man.

Patrick had another dream, full of Irish voices asking him to return to Ireland. He traveled back to the land where he had been a slave and was made Bishop of Ireland. Patrick traveled all over the island, and thousands turned away from their old pagan ways. He ordained priests and built many churches and monasteries. By the end of his life Patrick had converted almost all of Ireland.

One day, the two daughters of the pagan high-king asked Patrick the meaning of the Trinity. Saint Patrick picked up a shamrock and said that just as the shamrock has three leaves, God was three in one too.

Patrick is the patron saint of Ireland.

Saint Scholastica & Saint Benedict

SIXTH CENTURY

Benedict grew up in a noble family and studied in Rome, but he grew tired of the lack of discipline. He found a cave and lived as a hermit for three years. A raven reportedly brought him food.

Students came to him, and he was asked to be abbot of a monastery. Saint Benedict's great achievement was to write a Rule for the monastic way of life. Along with prayers and services, the monks were expected to do some sort of manual labor. Saint Benedict believed that physical work was good for the soul, and that it was not just for servants but for the noble-born as well. "Pray and work" was his motto.

Saint Benedict cured the sick, comforted the distressed, and gave assistance to the poor. Once during a famine he gave away all the bread in the monastery. He told the monks not to worry. Miraculously, on the following day, two hundred bushels of flour were left at the monastery gate.

Scholastica was Benedict's twin sister. A humble and devout nun, she was in charge of teaching a group of nuns not far from his monastery. At their last meeting, she begged him to stay an extra day to discuss the joys of heaven. When he refused, she prayed for rain. Such a storm arose that he could not travel, and so she had her wish. "What you have refused to me, God has granted," she told him. The next day Benedict returned home. Three days later he saw a vision of his sister's soul in the shape of a dove, and he knew she had died.

Scholastica is the patron saint of Benedictine nuns.

Saint Genevieve

SIXTH CENTURY

A seven-year-old girl was picked out of a crowd by Bishop Saint Germain in a small village near Paris. He took her parents aside and foretold of her future holiness.

Genevieve was presented to the Bishop of Paris when she was fifteen and took on the habit of a nun. She made many journeys for the sake of charity, and everywhere she went she worked miracles and made remarkable predictions.

Many people were suspicious of young Genevieve's gifts and hatefully accused her of all sorts of evil deeds. Her enemies wanted to discredit her and even plotted to drown her. However, Bishop Saint Germain shamed them all by visiting her publicly and treating her with great respect.

When the people of Paris heard that the brutal armies of Attila the Hun were on the march, they were ready to desert the city. Saint Genevieve persuaded them to avert the attack. "Pray and fast," she told the people, "and God will save our city." She spent many days along with other women in the baptistry of Paris, praying for the protection of heaven. And miraculously, the barbarian Attila changed course, leaving Paris untouched.

Genevieve spent her life caring for others. She often convinced the king of Paris to release prisoners, and she was such a miracle-worker that many people joined the Church. After her death, many cures were reported at her tomb. When her shrine was carried around Paris during a horrible epidemic, the dying got well and no others fell ill.

Genevieve is the patron saint of Paris.

Saint Brigid

There are differing accounts of Brigid's childhood in Ireland, one being that she was born to a slave. When her mother was sold to a pagan Druid priest, Brigid was included in the price. She tended the cows and helped with the farm chores. Whenever she had free time, she loved to wander in the forest and reportedly made friends with all sorts of animals, even a fierce wild boar.

Brigid often took food and goods from her master and gave them to the poor. Exasperated, he tried to sell her to the king of Leinster. When the king asked her to explain her actions, Brigid said, "God will reward with heavenly gifts those who give away worldly things." The king was a Christian and understood. He gave her master a jewel-encrusted sword, and Brigid was freed.

Brigid became a nun and later founded a religious community called the Church of the Oak. She contributed greatly to the spread of Christianity and was loved and honored by the people.

Saint Brigid was a miracle-worker of great power, and many people were healed by her prayers. She was famous for her hospitality and seemed to be able to multiply food to meet a need. When visitors appeared, the cows gave extra milk and tubs of water became beer. Brigid was gentle, humble, and forgiving. Though she was abbess of a monastery, she worked in the fields, tended the cows, made butter, and helped to harvest the corn.

Brigid lived to an old age. After her death a fire was kept burning at her shrine continuously for centuries, tended by the nuns of her community. She is a patron saint of Ireland.

Saint Columba

SIXTH CENTURY

Columba was a poet and bard with a voice so loud and melodious it was said it could be heard from a mile away. He became a priest and a great scholar who collected manuscripts and books. For fifteen years Columba traveled around Ireland, preaching and founding monasteries. Then he set out with twelve companions in a wicker boat covered with leather, landing on the island of Iona. There he built a monastery which was his home for the rest of his life and the base from which he evangelized the Scottish people.

Columba traveled to the castle of the Scottish king, who, being a pagan, had the gates barred against him. Columba made the sign of the cross, and the bolts opened. Columba boldly entered the castle. The king held Columba in high honor after this event and allowed him to preach to the people freely.

Columba was visited at Iona by many people needing healing, both physical and spiritual. In his later years he spent a great deal of time copying manuscripts and Bibles by hand, for there were no printing presses in those times.

The day before his death Columba was resting on a stump, and his favorite horse, a white pack horse, came up to him. Sensing that Columba was soon to die, the horse lowered its head onto his breast, and tears streamed from its eyes. The saint passed into eternal rest on that very night. The last thing that Columba wrote were the words, "They that love the Lord shall lack no good thing."

Columba is a patron saint of Scotland and Ireland.

Saint Mary of Egypt

FIFTH CENTURY

At the young age of twelve, Mary ran away from home and traveled to Alexandria. There she lived a life of sin and shame and caused others to commit evil deeds as well. One day she decided to go with a group making a pilgrimage to Jerusalem for the feast of the Holy Cross.

As Mary reached the doors of the church, some invisible force barred her way. She remained outside and wept bitterly, for she realized that her wicked life had prevented her from entering. She knelt before an icon of the Mother of God at the church's doorway and asked for her help. Her prayers were heard, and she entered the church and venerated the Holy Cross.

Soon after, Mary heard a voice instructing her to cross the Jordan River. Mary obeyed the voice and lived alone in the desert wilderness for the next forty-seven years. An elderly monk named Zosimas came upon her in the desert and was impressed by her holiness. She told him her amazing story. She had never learned to read or write, but she could quote from the scriptures, for the angels were her teachers. She lived on plants that grew in the desert.

Zosimas returned to Mary in one year and brought her holy communion. The following year he found that she had died. After the monk chanted hymns and prayers, a lion appeared and dug her grave, for the ground was too hard for the aged monk. Before he died, Zosimas told the story of Mary of Egypt so that she would always be remembered.

Saint Gregory the Great

SEVENTH CENTURY

When Gregory was abbot of Saint Andrew's in Rome, he saw some young slaves in the marketplace that impressed him greatly. When he asked who they were, he was told, "Angles," because they were Anglo-Saxons. "They look like angels, indeed," he responded. Gregory became determined to bring the light of Christianity to the Anglo-Saxon lands that are now England.

Gregory was unable to lead the expedition himself. Soon after he was elected Pope, an outbreak of plague kept him in Rome.

Finally, Gregory sent a group of monks to evangelize England, lead by the monk Augustine (who became a saint as well). He gave directions, encouragement, and support to their endeavors, and his writings were influential in their work.

Gregory was also busy on other fronts. He negotiated a peace treaty after an invasion of the Arian Lombards had laid waste half the land in Italy. He managed to convert them and then proceeded to win over the Spanish and French Goths.

Gregory wrote a number of books. His most popular, called *Dialogue*, contained stories of the lives of the saints. A collection of 854 letters by Gregory contains his thoughts on the problems of Church and State. Always a humble man, Gregory preferred to be known as "the servant of the servants of God."

After Gregory's death, the Church considered him one of the four great Doctors of the Church and gave him the title "Gregory the Great."

Saint Eloi

Eloi was apprenticed to a goldsmith when he was a young man and quickly showed a talent for the craft. He was commissioned to make a golden throne for the king of Paris. With the gold and precious stones allotted for one throne, Eloi used a clever design and made two thrones. The king was so impressed that he made Eloi master of the royal mint. There he designed coins, made crosses and chalices, and decorated tombs and shrines.

Eloi did not let his high station in life corrupt him. He grew very wealthy and dressed in silk embroidered with gold and gemstones, but he also used his wealth to help the poor. His house was easy to find. It always had a crowd of poor people in front of it, for every day he fed a great number of people in his own home.

If Eloi heard that slaves were to be sold, he went and ransomed fifty or a hundred at a time and set them free. He also used his wealth to build a monastery near Limoges and turned his house in Paris into a nunnery.

Eloi became a priest and was then made a bishop and served in Noyon. He was responsible for converting great numbers of people in Flanders. Every Easter he would baptize those to whom he had taught the faith in the previous year.

Eloi continued to practice his art all his life, using the money he received to aid the poor. He is the patron saint of farriers, metalworkers, and jewelers.

Saint Kevin

SEVENTH CENTURY

Kevin was born in Ireland. His nickname was Kevin of the Angels, for angels were seen around the font when he was baptized. At age seven, he was sent to school in a monastery.

After studying with the monks for many years, Kevin was ordained a priest. Feeling the need to retreat from the world for a time to meditate and pray, he settled in the wild upper reaches of the Valley of the Two Lakes, called Glendalough. There Kevin lived as a hermit for seven years, eating only berries, nuts, and wild plants.

Kevin loved the animals and birds that lived in the wilderness, and many of them approached him without fear. Once he dropped his prayer book into the lake, and an otter swam up from the depths with the book in its mouth. Not a letter was blurred. Then an angel appeared to Kevin and told him it was time for him to return to society to preach and teach the word of God.

Kevin resisted the angel's message. His health grew weaker, until he was discovered by a farmer whose cow strayed from the herd each day and stayed to lick Kevin's feet. The farmer took him home, and Kevin began to teach his family. Soon word spread of his wisdom, and people began to flock to the small farm. It was not long before they built a school, then added building after building, until Kevin's monastery at Glendalough became truly famous.

Once when food was scarce, Kevin's otter brought him salmon to feed his monks. Another time a blackbird laid an egg in Kevin's outstretched hand while he was praying, and Kevin did not move his hand until the egg hatched. Kevin reportedly lived to be one hundred and twenty years old.

Saint Brendan

Brendan was born to a family on the seacoast of Ireland. When he was but a baby, the bishop of the area came and claimed Brendan as a foster son. Brendan's first five years were spent in the care of Saint Ita at a convent school.

The bishop then took Brendan to his primitive monastery on the coast. He spent the next fourteen years living in a little stone beehive-shaped hut, studying, fishing, and farming. He loved the ocean and longed to seek out fabled, mysterious lands.

When Brendan was thirty, he was ordained a priest and could resist the call of the sea no longer. With fourteen companions he set sail and began the famous voyages for which he is called Brendan the Navigator.

Once, on the feast of Saint Paul, Brendan was at sea chanting prayers quite enthusiastically. One of his comrades said, "Sing more softly, Father, or we may be shipwrecked." He pointed to the water where all sorts of strange fish and sea creatures—some huge and fierce-looking—were swimming along with the boat.

Brendan laughed and said, "Where is your faith? Fear nothing but God. There is no danger here." Brendan continued to sing, and the creatures of the deep leapt around the boat on all sides, celebrating the joy of the feast. Then, they went on their way.

Brendan and his companions visited many remote places. It is even possible that he spent time in the Americas, seven hundred years before Columbus.

When Brendan returned to Ireland, he was made a bishop and spent years on land, building churches, teaching religion, and, of course, navigation. But he always went back to the sea.

Brendan is the patron saint of sailors.

Saint Bede

Unlike other saints who traveled to spread the word of God, Bede was content to stay in one place for his entire life. He said in his own words, "It has always been my delight to learn or to teach or to write." And Bede was a great success at all three.

Bede grew up on the lands of Saints Peter and Paul monastery in England, and when he was seven he moved into the monastery itself. At nineteen he was ordained a deacon, and at thirty he became a priest. He spent his time in prayer and study. He studied all the sciences, all types of literature, and mathematics. He studied the scriptures and was familiar with Latin, Hebrew, and Greek.

In order to teach all that he had learned to others, Bede began to write books, gathering together bits of information and writings from many different sources into his own words.

Bede became the first English historian. He wrote about the history of the Church in England. He wrote about the lives of the Anglo-Saxon saints and composed many different writings on the scriptures. He compiled books on music, medicine, philosophy, physics, and arithmetic. Bede also wrote about nature and poetry. He wrote forty-five works in all, an enormous accomplishment.

Because of his great learning and wisdom, after his death the Church bestowed upon him the title of the Venerable Bede, and he was declared the only English Doctor of the Church.

Bede is the patron saint of scholars.

Saint Theodora

In the year 829, the most beautiful girls from all parts of the Byzantine Empire were summoned to Constantinople. The new Emperor, Theophilus, needed a bride.

The bride he chose was Theodora. The Emperor presented the attractive girl with a golden apple. He did not realize that behind her beautiful face was an independent mind.

Theodora did not agree with many of her husband's policies. He had continued his father's policy of persecuting people who possessed icons, paintings of Christ and the saints. He and many other people believed that the veneration and praying in front of icons was a form of idol worship. Other people, including Theodora, believed that it was the person depicted on the icon that was venerated, not the wood and paint.

For the thirteen years that her husband was in power, Theodora kept icons hidden. She took them out when she was alone and prayed before them. Once one of her children saw her and asked what she was doing. "Mommy is just playing with her dolls," said Theodora. The child told the emperor that Mother played with dolls, just like she did. The emperor was angry, but Theodora hid the icons very well and they were not found.

When her husband died, Theodora ruled until her young son, Michael, was old enough to take the throne. She called a meeting of bishops, and they voted to restore the icons to the churches. She freed all those who had been imprisoned for possessing icons.

Theodora's victory is commemorated in the Orthodox Church on the first Sunday of Lent.

Saint Edmund

Edmund became king of East Anglia when he was fifteen years old. He served peacefully for another fifteen years, helping poor widows and children, punishing criminals, and in every way behaving as a model Christian. Then the peaceful times ended.

The Vikings invaded England with an army of ships, burning and plundering and killing. They especially sought to kill priests, monks, and nuns, and burned many churches and monasteries. A Viking named Ivar rowed to East Anglia and started to lay waste everything in his path. Edmund's forces met the invaders, but they were too small in number, and the king had to retreat.

Ivar sent a message to Edmund, saying that if the king agreed to surrender, he would accept the king as his vassal. Edmund decided he would rather die for his country than serve under such a cruel, godless war-leader. He refused to surrender or to flee.

Edmund waited in his castle for the advancing army. He threw down his weapons, wishing to follow Christ's example. Ivar's men dragged Edmund outside and tied him to a tree. After they beat him with rods, they shot him with arrows. Then, Ivar ordered the noble king beheaded. On the way back to their ship, Ivar's men threw his head into the woods to hide it, to insult and dishonor him, so that it could not be buried along with his body.

When Edmund's people came out of hiding, they searched for his head and found that it was guarded against other wild animals by a great, grey wolf. After he was buried, many miracles were reported at his grave, and when the Viking invasions were past, a church was built on the spot.

Edmund is the patron saint of kings, torture victims, and wolves.

Saint Maud

TENTH CENTURY

Maud was raised by her grandmother, who was abbess of a convent in Germany. Her parents arranged her marriage to Henry the Fowler, who became Duke of Saxony. He then went on to become King of Germany, and Maud became Queen.

While her husband was seeing to the security of the country by waging battles against their enemies, Queen Maud was busy waging war on poverty and spiritual illness. She comforted the sick, fed and instructed the poor, and visited prisoners. If those in prison were truly repentant of their crime, she sought to have them freed. Her husband was highly supportive of her works of charity.

The king and queen were married for twenty years and had three sons. When the king died, Maud cut off the jewels she was wearing and gave them to the priest, for she had no more desire for the things of this world. She continued to spend her wealth on the poor. She visited the sick and convinced criminals to mend their ways.

Two of her sons, Otho and Henry, succeeded in stripping her of all her property and money, saying that she had spent too much money belonging to the State on the poor. Finally, after many years and many bitter words, they repented and returned everything to her.

Making up for lost time, Maud proceeded to have many churches and monasteries built. At one time she supported over three thousand monks. The queen was a tireless worker and continued with her good works until her death.

Saint Dunstan

TENTH CENTURY

Dunstan grew up near Glastonbury in England. His uncle, a bishop, encouraged him to enter the monastic life and the priesthood. Dunstan built a small cell near the church in Glastonbury, spending his time in prayer and fasting and various crafts.

Dunstan was very talented with his hands. He made bells, crosses, and censers. He copied books and illuminated them with paintings. Dunstan was also quite musical and composed hymns. He often played the harp while the nuns embroidered his designs. Once, after he had put away his harp, the music continued, as if being played by the angels.

Dunstan was appointed Abbot of Glastonbury by King Edmund. Dunstan worked hard to renew monastic life in England, for it had been all but wiped out by the Viking invasions and hostile local authorities. He oversaw the reconstruction of a large abbey and restored the Church of Saint Peter. This abbey became a great school of learning, and Dunstan attracted many disciples.

Dunstan became Archbishop of Canterbury and from that position he was able to enact reforms in many churches and monasteries throughout England. He traveled far and wide, preaching and instructing the faithful. He was a miracle-worker and also was gifted with visions and prophecies.

Acting as a teacher, judge, and priest, Dunstan stayed active until the time of his death at about the age of eighty. Dunstan is the patron saint of jewelers, goldsmiths, and musicians.

Index of Saints